MY INFO

NAME:

NICKNAMES:

AGE:

THINGS I LIKE DOING:

MY BEST MATES:

MY MINECRAFT NAMERTAG:

MY FAVOURITE MINECRAFTERS:

WHY USE THIS BOOK?

IT'S A BUMPER EDITION! EVEN MORE PAGES TO DO ALL OF THE BELOW

Make better Minecraft worlds!

In a game of so much freedom, learn to set yourself different challenges to focus your efforts and achieve success!

Remember what you've learnt so you can progress more quickly

Show your parents how being a Minecrafter can be good for your education… it teaches you planning and organising, creativity and storytelling, innovation, technology skills, maths and science skills, engineering skills. How could they refuse?

If you choose to make epic YouTube videos of your Minecraft adventures and get lots of subscribers, you can start to make money!

ISBN: 978-1-912293-12-4

BEFORE YOU START:

Learn how to mine! You will need to learn the basics of Minecraft before you can really get going. **Mine wood** as with this you can make shelter, build things, make weapons to protect yourself, and fuel fire to cook food, keep warm and keep yourself alive.

Learn how to use the **crafting table.** Once you have collected logs of wood in your inventory you can make 4 wooden planks and create a crafting table. This is one of the most important things to have as allows you to collect different materials and make things with them.

Learn how to **survive!** If you are playing in survival mode you will need to make weapons, build a shelter and look out for monsters at night-time. Crafting torches also helps as the light stops monsters spawning near you.

Get creative! If you choose to play in creative mode, monsters can't see you and you will have all the blocs you need to get creative. You can choose to build anything you like.

Don't forget **SAFETY.** Your computer settings may allow other people to want to join your game. Remember people can be good or bad, kind or mean. Keep your personal information (real name, age, address, school) private. Discuss with your parents if you should play online or offline.

IDEAS TO START WITH...

SOME CHALLENGES TO GET YOU STARTED:

In Survival Mode:

👍 Gather some wood and make a crafting table. ☐

👍 Make some survival gear: a sword, a torch, and a pick-axe ☐

👍 Make some food; find and collect 3 x wheat and make it into bread on the crafting table ☐

👍 Build a house with stairs and a protective roof. Include a bedroom with a bed for night-time. Don't forget a door to keep mobs out. ☐

👍 Survive at night-time - fight off any monsters that appear or stay in your bed. ☐

In Creative mode:

👍 Build a track and cart and make a roller-coaster style ride. ☐

👍 Build houses and fields; make a village with crops for food and houses for shelter. ☐

👍 With another player, set up a game of hide and seek, Remember to turn namer tags off. ☐

👍 Build a swimming pool. ☐

👍 Make a rocket. ☐

NOW LET'S GET YOU STARTED >

MINECRAFT SKILLS BANK

As you play Minecraft more and more you will learn how to craft different tools. Use this page to note down the things you've learnt to make your own personal skills bank so you can remember them for next time and share with friends:

Build a torch =
1 × coal + 1 stick.
Use the crafting table

MINECRAFT SKILLS BANK

HANDY HINTS

CHALLENGE INDEX

Use this to keep a record of the challenges you want to do

Challenge Number	Challenge Title	Tactics
Example	*Build a den with an underground cellar*	*Make a shovel to dig with a stone block and 2 sticks. Use wood blocks for the den.*
1		
2		
3		
4		
5		
6		
7		
8		
9		
10		
11		
12		
13		
14		
15		
16		
17		

Top tip! Think about what you've seen other people do and then add something new!

Challenge Number	Challenge Title	Tactics
18		
19		
20		
21		
22		
23		
24		
25		
26		
27		
28		
29		
30		

MINECRAFT CHALLENGE NO. 1

Minecraft Mode:
Survival / Creative

What challenge do I want to do?

_____

_____

What will I need to craft?
And what materials will I need?

_____

_____

_____

_____

_____

_____

_____

_____

_____

What will be the hardest part of the challenge?

_____

Who will be interested in this challenge?
What will they like about it?

_____

_____

_____

_____

SUCCESS?

Did I succeed at this challenge? Yes / No

Date achieved: _____

What new Minecraft skills did I learn?

_____

_____

_____

How could I make it better next time?

_____

_____

MINECRAFT CHALLENGE NO. 2

Minecraft Mode:
Survival / Creative

What challenge do I want to do?

_____

_____

What will I need to craft?
And what materials will I need?

_____

_____

_____

_____

_____

_____

_____

What will be the hardest part of the challenge?

_____

Who will be interested in this challenge?
What will they like about it?

_____

_____

_____

_____

SuCCESS?

Did I succeed at this challenge? Yes / No

Date achieved: _____

What new Minecraft skills did I learn?

_____

_____

_____

How could I make it better next time?

_____

_____

MINECRAFT CHALLENGE NO. 3

Minecraft Mode:
Survival / Creative

What challenge do I want to do?

_____

_____

What will I need to craft?
And what materials will I need?

_____

_____

_____

_____

_____

_____

_____

_____

What will be the hardest part of the challenge?

_____

Who will be interested in this challenge?
What will they like about it?

_____

_____

_____

_____

SUCCESS?

Did I succeed at this challenge? Yes / No

Date achieved: _____

What new Minecraft skills did I learn?

_____

_____

_____

How could I make it better next time?

_____

_____

MINECRAFT CHALLENGE NO. 4

Minecraft Mode:
Survival / Creative

What challenge do I want to do?

_____

_____

What will I need to craft?
And what materials will I need?

_____

_____

_____

_____

_____

_____

_____

What will be the hardest part of the challenge?

_____

Who will be interested in this challenge?
What will they like about it?

_____

_____

_____

SUCCESS?

Did I succeed at this challenge? Yes / No

Date achieved: _____

What new Minecraft skills did I learn?

_____

_____

_____

How could I make it better next time?

_____

_____

MINECRAFT CHALLENGE NO. 5

Minecraft Mode:
Survival / Creative

What challenge do I want to do?

_____

_____

What will I need to craft?
And what materials will I need?

_____

_____

_____

_____

_____

_____

_____

What will be the hardest part of the challenge?

_____

Who will be interested in this challenge?
What will they like about it?

_____

_____

_____

_____

SUCCESS?

Did I succeed at this challenge? Yes / No

Date achieved: _____

What new Minecraft skills did I learn?

_____

_____

_____

How could I make it better next time?

_____

_____

MINECRAFT CHALLENGE NO. 6

Minecraft Mode:
Survival / Creative

What challenge do I want to do?

_____

_____

What will I need to craft?
And what materials will I need?

_____

_____

_____

_____

_____

_____

_____

What will be the hardest part of the challenge?

_____

Who will be interested in this challenge?
What will they like about it?

_____

_____

_____

_____

SUCCESS?

Did I succeed at this challenge? Yes / No

Date achieved: _____

What new Minecraft skills did I learn?

_____

_____

_____

How could I make it better next time?

_____

_____

MINECRAFT CHALLENGE NO. 7

Minecraft Mode:
Survival / Creative

What challenge do I want to do?

_____

_____

What will I need to craft?
And what materials will I need?

_____

_____

_____

_____

_____

_____

_____

_____

What will be the hardest part of the challenge?

_____

Who will be interested in this challenge?
What will they like about it?

_____

_____

_____

_____

SUCCESS?

Did I succeed at this challenge? Yes / No

Date achieved: _____

What new Minecraft skills did I learn?

_____

_____

_____

How could I make it better next time?

_____

_____

MINECRAFT CHALLENGE NO. 8

Minecraft Mode:
Survival / Creative

What challenge do I want to do?

_____

_____

What will I need to craft?
And what materials will I need?

_____

_____

_____

_____

_____

_____

_____

What will be the hardest part of the challenge?

_____

Who will be interested in this challenge?
What will they like about it?

_____

_____

_____

_____

SuccESS?

Did I succeed at this challenge? Yes / No

Date achieved: _____

What new Minecraft skills did I learn?

_____

_____

_____

How could I make it better next time?

_____

_____

MINECRAFT CHALLENGE NO. 9

Minecraft Mode:
Survival / Creative

What challenge do I want to do?

_____

_____

What will I need to craft?
And what materials will I need?

_____

_____

_____

_____

_____

_____

_____

What will be the hardest part of the challenge?

_____

Who will be interested in this challenge?
What will they like about it?

_____

_____

_____

_____

SUCCESS?

Did I succeed at this challenge? Yes / No

Date achieved: _____

What new Minecraft skills did I learn?

_____

_____

_____

How could I make it better next time?

_____

_____

MINECRAFT CHALLENGE NO. 10

Minecraft Mode:
Survival / Creative

What challenge do I want to do?

_____

_____

What will I need to craft?
And what materials will I need?

_____

_____

_____

_____

_____

_____

_____

What will be the hardest part of the challenge?

_____

Who will be interested in this challenge?
What will they like about it?

_____

_____

_____

_____

SUCCESS?

Did I succeed at this challenge? Yes / No

Date achieved: _____

What new Minecraft skills did I learn?

_____

_____

_____

How could I make it better next time?

_____

_____

MINECRAFT CHALLENGE NO. 11

Minecraft Mode:
Survival / Creative

What challenge do I want to do?

_____

_____

What will I need to craft?
And what materials will I need?

_____

_____

_____

_____

_____

_____

_____

_____

What will be the hardest part of the challenge?

_____

Who will be interested in this challenge?
What will they like about it?

_____

_____

_____

_____

SUCCESS?

Did I succeed at this challenge? Yes / No

Date achieved: _____

What new Minecraft skills did I learn?

_____

_____

_____

How could I make it better next time?

_____

_____

MINECRAFT CHALLENGE NO. 12

Minecraft Mode:
Survival / Creative

What challenge do I want to do?

_____

_____

What will I need to craft?
And what materials will I need?

_____

_____

_____

_____

_____

_____

_____

What will be the hardest part of the challenge?

_____

Who will be interested in this challenge?
What will they like about it?

_____

_____

_____

SUCCESS?

Did I succeed at this challenge? Yes / No

Date achieved: _____

What new Minecraft skills did I learn?

_____

_____

_____

How could I make it better next time?

_____

_____

MINECRAFT CHALLENGE NO. 13

Minecraft Mode:
Survival / Creative

What challenge do I want to do?

_____

_____

What will I need to craft?
And what materials will I need?

_____

_____

_____

_____

_____

_____

_____

What will be the hardest part of the challenge?

_____

Who will be interested in this challenge?
What will they like about it?

_____

_____

_____

_____

SUCCESS?

Did I succeed at this challenge? Yes / No

Date achieved: _____

What new Minecraft skills did I learn?

_____

_____

_____

How could I make it better next time?

_____

_____

MINECRAFT CHALLENGE NO. 14

Minecraft Mode:
Survival / Creative

What challenge do I want to do?

_____

_____

What will I need to craft?
And what materials will I need?

_____

_____

_____

_____

_____

_____

_____

_____

What will be the hardest part of the challenge?

_____

Who will be interested in this challenge?
What will they like about it?

_____

_____

_____

SuCCESS?

Did I succeed at this challenge? Yes / No

Date achieved: _____

What new Minecraft skills did I learn?

_____

_____

_____

How could I make it better next time?

_____

_____

MINECRAFT CHALLENGE NO. 15

Minecraft Mode:
Survival / Creative

What challenge do I want to do?

_____

_____

What will I need to craft?
And what materials will I need?

_____

_____

_____

_____

_____

_____

_____

What will be the hardest part of the challenge?

_____

Who will be interested in this challenge?
What will they like about it?

_____

_____

_____

_____

Success?

Did I succeed at this challenge? Yes / No

Date achieved: _____

What new Minecraft skills did I learn?

_____

_____

_____

How could I make it better next time?

_____

_____

MINECRAFT CHALLENGE NO. 16

Minecraft Mode:
Survival / Creative

What challenge do I want to do?

_____

_____

What will I need to craft?
And what materials will I need?

_____

_____

_____

_____

_____

_____

_____

What will be the hardest part of the challenge?

_____

Who will be interested in this challenge?
What will they like about it?

_____

_____

_____

Success?

Did I succeed at this challenge? Yes / No

Date achieved: _____

What new Minecraft skills did I learn?

_____

_____

_____

How could I make it better next time?

_____

_____

MINECRAFT CHALLENGE NO. 17

Minecraft Mode:
Survival / Creative

What challenge do I want to do?

_____

_____

What will I need to craft?
And what materials will I need?

_____

_____

_____

_____

_____

_____

_____

What will be the hardest part of the challenge?

_____

Who will be interested in this challenge?
What will they like about it?

_____

_____

_____

_____

Success?

Did I succeed at this challenge? Yes / No

Date achieved: _____

What new Minecraft skills did I learn?

_____

_____

_____

How could I make it better next time?

_____

_____

MINECRAFT CHALLENGE NO. 18

Minecraft Mode:
Survival / Creative

What challenge do I want to do?

_____

_____

What will I need to craft?
And what materials will I need?

_____

_____

_____

_____

_____

_____

_____

What will be the hardest part of the challenge?

_____

Who will be interested in this challenge?
What will they like about it?

_____

_____

_____

_____

SUCCESS?

Did I succeed at this challenge? Yes / No

Date achieved: _____

What new Minecraft skills did I learn?

_____

_____

_____

How could I make it better next time?

_____

_____

MINECRAFT CHALLENGE NO. 19

Minecraft Mode:
Survival / Creative

What challenge do I want to do?

_____

_____

What will I need to craft?
And what materials will I need?

_____

_____

_____

_____

_____

_____

_____

_____

What will be the hardest part of the challenge?

_____

Who will be interested in this challenge?
What will they like about it?

_____

_____

_____

_____

SUCCESS?

Did I succeed at this challenge? Yes / No

Date achieved: _____

What new Minecraft skills did I learn?

_____

_____

_____

How could I make it better next time?

_____

_____

MINECRAFT CHALLENGE NO. 20

Minecraft Mode:
Survival / Creative

What challenge do I want to do?

_____

_____

What will I need to craft?
And what materials will I need?

_____

_____

_____

_____

_____

_____

What will be the hardest part of the challenge?

_____

Who will be interested in this challenge?
What will they like about it?

_____

_____

_____

SUCCESS?

Did I succeed at this challenge? Yes / No

Date achieved: _____

What new Minecraft skills did I learn?

_____

_____

_____

How could I make it better next time?

_____

_____

MINECRAFT CHALLENGE NO. 21

Minecraft Mode:
Survival / Creative

What challenge do I want to do?

_____

_____

What will I need to craft?
And what materials will I need?

_____

_____

_____

_____

_____

_____

_____

_____

What will be the hardest part of the challenge?

_____

Who will be interested in this challenge?
What will they like about it?

_____

_____

_____

Success?

Did I succeed at this challenge? Yes / No

Date achieved: _____

What new Minecraft skills did I learn?

_____

_____

_____

How could I make it better next time?

_____

_____

MINECRAFT CHALLENGE NO. 22

Minecraft Mode:
Survival / Creative

What challenge do I want to do?

_____

_____

What will I need to craft?
And what materials will I need?

_____

_____

_____

_____

_____

_____

_____

What will be the hardest part of the challenge?

_____

Who will be interested in this challenge?
What will they like about it?

_____

_____

_____

SUCCESS?

Did I succeed at this challenge? Yes / No

Date achieved: _____

What new Minecraft skills did I learn?

_____

_____

How could I make it better next time?

_____

_____

MINECRAFT CHALLENGE NO. 23

Minecraft Mode:
Survival / Creative

What challenge do I want to do?

_____

_____

What will I need to craft?
And what materials will I need?

_____

_____

_____

_____

_____

_____

_____

_____

What will be the hardest part of the challenge?

_____

Who will be interested in this challenge?
What will they like about it?

_____

_____

_____

SUCCESS?

Did I succeed at this challenge? Yes / No

Date achieved: _____

What new Minecraft skills did I learn?

_____

_____

_____

How could I make it better next time?

_____

_____

MINECRAFT CHALLENGE NO. 24

Minecraft Mode:
Survival / Creative

What challenge do I want to do?

_____

_____

What will I need to craft?
And what materials will I need?

_____

_____

_____

_____

_____

_____

_____

What will be the hardest part of the challenge?

_____

Who will be interested in this challenge?
What will they like about it?

_____

_____

_____

_____

SUCCESS?

Did I succeed at this challenge? Yes / No

Date achieved: _____

What new Minecraft skills did I learn?

_____

_____

_____

How could I make it better next time?

_____

_____

MINECRAFT CHALLENGE NO. 25

Minecraft Mode:
Survival / Creative

What challenge do I want to do?

_____

_____

What will I need to craft?
And what materials will I need?

_____

_____

_____

_____

_____

_____

_____

_____

What will be the hardest part of the challenge?

_____

Who will be interested in this challenge?
What will they like about it?

_____

_____

_____

SUCCESS?

Did I succeed at this challenge? Yes / No

Date achieved: _____

What new Minecraft skills did I learn?

_____

_____

_____

How could I make it better next time?

_____

_____

MINECRAFT CHALLENGE NO. 26

Minecraft Mode:
Survival / Creative

What challenge do I want to do?

_____

_____

What will I need to craft?
And what materials will I need?

_____

_____

_____

_____

_____

_____

_____

What will be the hardest part of the challenge?

_____

Who will be interested in this challenge?
What will they like about it?

_____

_____

_____

SUCCESS?

Did I succeed at this challenge? Yes / No

Date achieved: _____

What new Minecraft skills did I learn?

_____

_____

_____

How could I make it better next time?

_____

_____

MINECRAFT CHALLENGE NO. 27

Minecraft Mode:
Survival / Creative

What challenge do I want to do?

_____

_____

What will I need to craft?
And what materials will I need?

_____

_____

_____

_____

_____

_____

_____

_____

What will be the hardest part of the challenge?

_____

Who will be interested in this challenge?
What will they like about it?

_____

_____

_____

SuCCESS?

Did I succeed at this challenge? Yes / No

Date achieved: _____

What new Minecraft skills did I learn?

_____

_____

_____

How could I make it better next time?

_____

_____

MINECRAFT CHALLENGE NO. 28

Minecraft Mode:
Survival / Creative

What challenge do I want to do?

_____

_____

What will I need to craft?
And what materials will I need?

_____

_____

_____

_____

_____

_____

_____

What will be the hardest part of the challenge?

_____

Who will be interested in this challenge?
What will they like about it?

_____

_____

_____

_____

SUCCESS?

Did I succeed at this challenge? Yes / No

Date achieved: _____

What new Minecraft skills did I learn?

_____

_____

_____

How could I make it better next time?

_____

_____

MINECRAFT CHALLENGE NO. 29

Minecraft Mode:
Survival / Creative

What challenge do I want to do?

_____

_____

What will I need to craft?
And what materials will I need?

_____

_____

_____

_____

_____

_____

_____

What will be the hardest part of the challenge?

_____

Who will be interested in this challenge?
What will they like about it?

_____

_____

_____

_____

SUCCESS?

Did I succeed at this challenge? Yes / No

Date achieved: _____

What new Minecraft skills did I learn?

_____

_____

_____

How could I make it better next time?

_____

_____

MINECRAFT CHALLENGE NO. 30

Minecraft Mode:
Survival / Creative

What challenge do I want to do?

_____

_____

What will I need to craft?
And what materials will I need?

_____

_____

_____

_____

_____

_____

_____

What will be the hardest part of the challenge?

_____

Who will be interested in this challenge?
What will they like about it?

_____

_____

_____

_____

SUCCESS?

Did I succeed at this challenge? Yes / No

Date achieved: _____

What new Minecraft skills did I learn?

_____

_____

_____

How could I make it better next time?

_____

_____

YOUTUBE INDEX + REVIEW

If you choose to post your challenges on YouTube you can keep a track of their success here:

Date	Challenge Title	Duration	Views / Likes / Comments / Shares
e.g. 02/07/17	Minecraft Challenge: Building lots of weapons	2m31s	14 Views, 10 Likes, 1 Comment, 0 Shares

Date	Video Title	Duration	Views / Likes / Comments / Shares

NOTES AND DOODLES

Made in the USA
Coppell, TX
18 November 2021

65972679R00042